NO TIGER

NO TIGER

MIKA

No Tiger

ISBN-13: 978-1-7335694-7-7
ISBN-10: 1-7335694-7-2

Cover design by Mike Corrao

www.apocalypse-party.com

Printed in the U.S.A

CONTENTS

Thanks to Vera for her contribution of the collage found on page 11 and her continually inspiring work. She tweets @knifebitch69 and maintains the project @iamvore.

Scalez 2717

half-lived girl, scaled curiosity decaying under sand /
wesley swift's fused radioactive green sand! the sinner
actualized in split atoms beginning with spine / great
periods of silence. except for winds with no flesh to flay.
breath of anthrax two times removed. not allowed to
become imprint on brick / not allowed to have ribcage
dusted / not allowed to have memory disintegrated
against a scabbed over-expanse of particles forming /
crumbling / reforming. glowstick fluid – cyalume – leaking
out of right eye. staining ground in liquid nightlights.
blunted perception / eye socket turning into home for
gamma mites. the inert weapon weeps charcoal – joy.

trash sea afloat / the plastic choking barracuda. humans
so good at killing they do it after they're all dead /
abomination-turned. civilizations buried underneath beer
cans. last remnants before they plunged beneath the Great
Pacific Garbage Heap. flesh / spirits free / the world our
self-actualization victim. she / lizard jacking off to collapse.
sludgecum on the emerald glass of a Texas beach. we finally
figured out what's hot or not. the decrepit remains of a
society hungry for more / more bodies until it needed to
eat all the bodies all at once. she needs bodies, bodies in
her, bodies all over her. super desire flowing out her venom
glands / prove herself / to god / girlhood can be earned.

resist survival / bite the hand that dares. lizard getting

fucked by one of the mites, sedan-sized / snap her vertebrate / that's okay. he's her boyfriend. it's okay. he only gets rough sometimes / good fuck. guro doujin actualized in this post-hell. skin rooting itself underneath a dirtsand blend. sheer off limbs he licks her emptied legs. / parasite lover / soulmate / protector he is. missing the acrid stench of pulled triggers. a fear in the veins passing with lurid movements. the blood is pink now / last surviving neon sign staining her teeth. live in the black jet. the mite picks up his limbless scaly gf. make a fucktopia / ridges on her breasts burnt like edges of a bullet hole. wounds full with her blood. her belly fat with sterile eggs. bursting chest open / the mucous numbing her guts / leaving her skin hot. brain swimming in endorphins. the insect king feasted well tonight.

she's illuminati now. no scumbags left to dominate the currency fetishists. all skeletons anyhow, burning red atop the New York Desert. lizard let anyone fuck her now. open gangbang invitation to all the terrors of the world / keep the diseased from erecting temples once more. offered up freely. slaughter of her insides / letting monster nails scrape her walls. making a new hole 10 degrees left her spinal cord. pour your thick isotopes into her chest cavity too / no holds barred. Paris beautiful. fuck her with depleted uranium sabots.

procession of sharks choking on bombarded fish background of her paradise. the wastefields. they call / sing / whisper / come here let me hold you. the wind is hungry, lizard trembles. coyote in grayscale wanders Arizona sands swarming like nanomachines / a lust. another beast to satisfy. threat level maximum. mite-boyfriend finally turned to ash / maladapted scorpions reduce down to baser particles in death valley. infinite tanks roll through hellscapes. armor on ever-rewinding feedback loops. the diamond treads chewing on femurs. hatred still alive / congealing skull-fluids. embrace the half-lived state. the only cock left to suck. deep-throating the decimating / puking up herself. after a point are you even dead anymore.

TRANSMUTATION OUTSIDE THE SHUTTERED HOME DEPOT

the self curated in outside sensory
i emerged from the depths of the plaster
in your basement walls, you wanted me!

i smell how you want
i look how you want
i act how you want

i fuck how you want
and because i'm not
made of what you want

you're still going to kill me how you want, aren't you

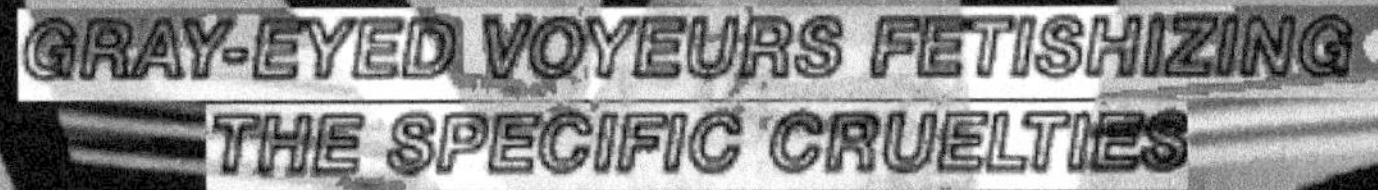
GRAY-EYED VOYEURS FETISHIZING
THE SPECIFIC CRUELTIES
IMPERIAL COMBUSTIONS FROM METAL
SERPENT TONGUES FITTED
W/ COMPENSATORS
THE DEVIL'S DESIGNATED AH-64
HELL WAS INVENTED IN 1975

BEING THE SEWAGE OF OUR SOCIETY IS MORE ENJOYABLE THAN IT MIGHT SEEM!

girls only! rest beneath the overpass
come sit with me, dredges that we are
copper behind our ears & silver grass
splitting gravel apart heavy water...
blood throbs in the cheeks,
geiger clicks.

life lives in the perpetual danger state
we only perceive in rose nowadays
that's okay, let lucidity gut me

cheap kills & fuck thrills & gold frills

reside the dumping ground
rejection evaporated thrash & thrash & thrash
its normal. i thrash weekly still
after the venusian rains local
to the highway's underbelly, fuck it!
keep speaking in aliases and
seducing taiga wolves
now there's tanks angled like daggers
slicing the mountainside
w/ a choker of barbed wire shredding
her throat into revolting ribbons—a whimper
"this underworld become our heaven, damn you"

mika eat your heart out bitch!

desperate to show the net how real
of a girl i can fucking be
organs wilted & perfumed in copper
i encounter Her

glare sheering off my arm at the elbow
gaze following the blood as it congeals
in the concrete dust

platinum grill clicked over her teeth
begging's the only way i know how
to give a damn anymore—girl, kick
those teeth in & relish shattered gums
gurgling out, eviscerated

this is my femininity:
gnashed metal & teeth lodged in my jaw
ready to fucking die for the Viral!
ready to fucking die for her Womanhood!

nicotine tossed over lungs death accelerant
day-to-day empty sonic booms
the sirens loose on my senses

in that sweet death spiral i'm lady in concept only
endless performances & chomping down on gray matter
static skull & sulfur bubblegum
what's left, who's to say mika ever was

tremors deep in the bone

graffitied nails, waxed eyes
the girl immerses in lead

slotted twin gazes together
in front of bathroom mirrors

under the december moon i drag daggers
against my temple
flesh turnt ash against the linoleum
strip myself down 'till all that's left is
the muscles vibrating at 20hz
veins pulsating in open air

fluorescents buzz in my head the light
soaks into the roots of my hair
clinging to fingertips like sewage
leaned over the bathtub edge
vomit-corroded throat seeping tarot
tracing out fortunes for you in the bile
they say nothing and please let me hold you

i'm still expelling crouched despair
wounds gushing interstate wide
on self-collision compression in
the soft parts of a bottom skull
i feel my face meld with the puke
2D blend flatlander resigned & hyenas cackle

yeah i'm coming down yeah i'm coming down
yeah i'm coming down

chernobyl taught me how to put on lipstick

i.   when the gamma rays wash over the landscape
i will have my arms outstretched
let my atoms be bombared until i'm black imprint on brick
rewrite the XY to XX distortions just in time
to suck teeth in defiance before
my eyes fall into layers of charcoal

ii.   smile for those nights you spend trying to
suffocate yourself against that make-believe body dissect
rearranged by invasive primal tongues as you
walk down the hot hallway
where the Elephant's Foot cooks engineers

fuck heave and fuck paradise
our nirvana is inside the concrete tomb
pulling the eaten landscape towards it

finger of either hand and a flick of the wrist,
practice in front of a mirror, skin so delicate
it can be punctured by a sliver, this serrated
blade is weighted for smaller hands, i keep
one in my purse and one in my cut from the
top of the pelvis to the diaphragm and pull,
any residual biomatter can be collected and
analyzed  by law
in the event of
an attack, this knife
could be a
gift for a wife or
daughter, Stainless
Steel with Mother of Pearl inlay grip, the
blood had dried into the cotton skirt, easy to
clean, carry, and place the severed head
between
the thighs, this jeweled blade i hold
firm to my breast, when i was cut
first the thin membrane gave way

GENERATION KILL CHIC

a black sun beats down
cracked meth pipes under boots
acrid bubbles of opossum roadkill pop
indiana's pretty this time of year

this teen keeps making others
grab him by his
curled devil horns – dealers like
feeling the scales they just
ripped outta his head one day like they were
full metal jackets shredding apart
fist-wide hole blown out
bloodfucked across bathwater

they'd give him extra oxy's when he
let em facefuck him
fingers dug in between keratin

liked the feeling like he was more
than the other boys were – as if he
was existing beyond capacity but still
once a week he would wake up
briefly afraid he was just
another boy like all the rest

he wanted to someday
drive an M2 Bradley fucking up all those

motherfucking terrorists just a little
maybe make a city burn down
just a little and
save the world just a little —

sometimes his daydreams would be invaded:
[atop takur ghar mountain he's bleeding out
& chest reorganized across the sand
amongst the erupted
insides he notices an unfamiliar chunk of
gore. knows he's less than
the other boys. not much of one
at all, really]

— he just wanted to be more
more & more until he didn't think anymore
even if that's by reducing
decades of proxy imperialism, and
corroding Powers That Be down
to the reverb of an M242 chain gun
turns skin to flesh to open bone

the mountains of afghanistan are pretty all year

echoes overlapping the 25mm's
fucking their way out the
end of a platinum barrel
stained with mudblood
twenty-seven tons of pure fucking power

the horns like a dead snake

a scorpion wanders – 0000 HOUR – in an
afghan valley – warmed in aftermath of
tracers in stuttered glow

so what if a few heads get popped?
so what if it was just for escape?
so what if he hated how much
he smelled like a boy?

so it's the last summer
directions for the
recruiting office on his desk a dealer arrived
the teen swallowed every time he hated the taste
tears clung to his cheek in throatfuck given a
tab of blotter paper with 1/25th's
a wolf head
for being so good and so hot and so girly
melted against his tongue
the fuck is this, he said

head began to churn his ego his id blended
reptile aspect human aspect turned
indifferent sludge pooling on back of tongue
blood drained out the nose the heart cleaned out
hollowpoint hallucination he's consumed
self diffracting along edges of a
fatal non-wound turning fractal

iridescence leaking out of him
what a vampiric chemical

castrated lust to feel a 7.62mm round
against his fingernail
immobilized desperation to feel the kick
of a TOW missile
vibrating the chassis
stilled drive to see red sand

the horns smoldered & cracked & blazed
until he was the only thing left

run away from the ghosts of
all those people you
never killed

denial cycles

girl born altered doomed a beast
the moon dies and

i'm not bleeding like i'm supposed to
voice deepening i speak in the stranger
each word pitched down backwards
forcing hexes in my skull

no amount of eyeliner makes
the blood come out where it should
crotch scabbed over
crimson sludge oozing
from all the wrong sewers
another moon dies like always

i just wanted to wear a dress
simple want a simple fantasy
dragged into a murdered heart

i claw the grass &
sink teeth into muscle
howling at the moon's dead body

false ichor sinking in the teeth and dirt
drink it like poison
guzzle at the wound
the moon dies over & over & over

her corpses begin to pile up in the corner and
all i do now is bleed heavy everyday
it won't stop the blood won't stop
i'm never going to be a mother, am i?

SHARKS

killed on surface level
half-ghosted atop the ocean
plastic waste dipping thru
my jellyfish body like yellowsnake
squeezing thru crude oil membrane
wanna see a tiger shark fuck me?
i dont have a choice so eat up
headsmashed & headrot & giving a barracuda head
asking that tiger dino freak bending me over
am i toxic am i hot am i pretty
his dick slides into abdomen
liver viscous wrapping around
the shark inside me
let fuckboys on their iphones
stream the hotness via drone feed
my slimesoft stomach getting plowed
buy my manyvids recording of it
i am a jell-o branded cam girl
his sewagejizz punches in
congealing
inside of aorta
now i'm cumming and it feels like
formatting leadbloated
harddrive brain by knifing
the skullback. yelling no no no
no no no no no no no
i think i liked it no oh no no

please do it again oh no
i'm letting myself sink just below
i dont have a choice anyways
surfacing w/ glass eyes

NEW UNIT
USURP UNIT

NEW DRONEPHASE
JOIN DRONEPHASE

OPTIONS
SAFEWORD XXXXXX

FLASHLAND

FLASHLAND

face flush to the screen until my eyes melt to the glass. ass pressed against the chair i begin to lose the sensations separating me & leather. i employ a macro to auto-click away 238 ad windows. tick tick tick mouse clicks fetter across my desk / *HOT PRE-USED CUM CORPSES BURIED NEAR U / LEARN SECRET 2 SUMMON A DAEMON 2 INSTA-GIB YOU & FUCK THE REMAINS NOW / 10 OCCULT WAYS THE WORLD IS ENDING AS YOU WALLOW HERE etc.*

at the desktop i start up **FLASHLAND.exe**. screen fills w/ white like a stun grenade just popped in my mouth. black fades in / splash logos zoom by / companies ive never heard of + Sierra / i get hard in anticipation. body already knows whats up by now. its the only time it gets to die. chipping my nail polish against the keyboard is like slathering my gums in coke, but i never seem to have enough & i never seem to need more than a taste to get sent off. the word **FLASHLAND** blares in cleansed white on the left. techno beats from the OST fucking each other in disharmony drops of blood leaking out my headphones every time, oh well.

the main menu options are laid out like this:
NEW UNIT
USURP UNIT
NEW DRONEPHASE

**JOIN DRONEPHASE
OPTIONS
SAFEWORD XXXXXX**
i click on **NEW UNIT**.

i don't know where i got ***FLASHLAND***. a transient program spectre that appeared on my desktop one day & fuck it! i wanted to see pics of my family torn apart w/ hyperrealistic blood or whatever anyway. probably something made by someone bored on 4chan, i thought. i start it at every dusk (it disappears like a tek vampire during daylight) & make a new file. if i don't... you ever get dope sick from a video game?

the ***FLASHLAND*** logo dissipates into metallic background & the animation of the flickering menu options trips over itself for a second as a formless vaguehuman flickers out of digital nothing into pure visual info. mass of the blackness between sewer grates. i am a mother. this is the womb i will shape this fucking stupid nothing into something & then at least temporarily murder myself just enough that me & my bastard kilobyte child are the same. there are a set of sliders oriented along the left side of the screen, in a neat column. getting to design me.

i wish there were more sliders. if i get to make their breasts large enough to snap their spine / if i get to make HER tall enough to turn me to a flat paste with their feet / i should be able to only let them be cursed with mild anxiety

/ i should be able to maximize HER self-esteem maybe. but really it has the only option that matters the false dichotomy. MALE or FEMALE, a third option necessary in our (falsely) neatly kept reality. i pick the latter. though i knew the only gender i really cared about was the position on the breast size slider. tits like sharpened lead, pyramids blurred. i spin the AVATAR (me) (this is myself i repeat on repeat) around using my mouse. trying to make myself sick with HER image. blur us together until i forget which one made who & i'm having my every movement dictated by a bitch clacking away on a keyboard. CUTE x5 fires like pistons in my head CUTE CUTE CUTE CUTE CUTE. cuteness slopping out my fogged eyeballs like gristle off rotting pig. i hit enter / main menu again / click on **NEW DRONEPHASE**. dick stirs underneath my panties.

a box w/ a loading bar centered in it—100×400 height/width—appears at the bottom of the screen. my char's / SHESHESHESHE / feet plant in smoothed over glass terrain of a monochrome desert. gray sand at my conjoined polygon toes. the soundtrack cuts out as soon as the game begins proper, i alt-tab out w/ the game window flinging black all over my monitor like glitching bukkake, over & over again, ugh. my computer calms its shit / i start spitting the word ***FLASHLAND*** down a search engine's throat until it chokes on overload / nothing. like the program was birthed directly out of the cunt in the back of my brain / my mind / stretched to uselessness as gigabyte ghosts squeezed out into my hardrive. **this playthrough is different.**

oh well! i alt-tab back into the game & make my screen
freak out a little more. glass desert. gray, again. monoliths
colored like snow coat lined oriented as twin parallels
forward, creating a path 7 characters wide until mist
slices down mid-way thru a set of pillars. fog wall defined
like razor edges. still, silent. blood still pouring out
my ears like someone's draining my skull & dripping
onto my shirt. i begin walking towards the knife sharp
fog wall. every prior session ended here / **.exe** would
slice apart / disappear off the desktop to some murky
folder buried within the recursive safeguards holding
stashes of anime girls cut to pieces. i continue / curious
to see what the doom at the end of this is all about.

i dont get more than 3 cells down the pathway until heat
searing the edges of the satin in my pants threatens to burn
a hole thru. i position HER against the corner of a pillar.
clawing my fingers together to get as many of the movement
keys pressed at once, i begin to grind HER crotch against
the corner / the general area around HER groin sliding
silently & sterilely / against flat polygons until i begin to
tingle feeling HER skin as my skin scraping / binary given
form. i don't know when my hand slipped under my skirt,
becoming my own out-of-body molestor, stroking my cock
to the view on screen jittering like the monitor edges would
crack under pressure. i don't know when it went all fever
pitch & i coated the edges of my skirt. my character gave
in too, falling into distinct pieces, dismembered against
the pillar corner / arms / legs / head / heart / bouncing as

giblets across the wasteland. my dick was all formless slime clinging against my thigh like a blood splatter. main menu:

NEW UNIT
NEW UNIT
NEW UNIT
NEW UNIT
NEW UNIT
NEW UNIT
NEW UNIT
NEW UNIT
JOIN DRONEPHASE

let my family be slaughtered. i want to cum again. i want HER *at all costs*. force feed me their blood for all i care. moving HER forward i reach a facsimile of a farmhouse on the right, a break in the pillar forest / a museum exhibit someone pretends to live in. windows glossed over w/ deeply held textures. i hit the faded E key as i approach the door **LOADING...**

no furniture / no lights but lit like a hospital / hallways held together by amateur code, thirsty to collapse HER into lost save file. thought it looked vaguely like my house / realized that's fucking stupid. the kitchen almost like a stock photo of a 50s nuclear family kitchen except none of the cupboards open, theres no table theres no fridge just an inoperable sink / no breadwinner man bleeding righteous terror. the bathroom won't open, nor the basement. a sound clip of a dog barking (0:09 seconds) loops continuously /

muffled spree murder emanating beneath the 5D / from outside the house. i keep forgetting what the inside of my room looks like. the blood keeps coming out my ears / i should have bled out by now / i keep playing. the periphery around my monitors begins to collapse down to the bluelight.

a scene: master bedroom. two discrete masses of triangles / fuck! / look at my parents. poorly rendered dummies flesh faces strapped on with digi-staples / murky copies of the Mother the Father / slathered deep blood/ bloodsheets001a / fake guts strewn on the bed. so hot! i feel HER shiver… sick with HER image… i move my hand down, i feel HER / **MY** sharply edged pussy shaped diamond / hand coated in wetness devoid physics, stuck to the featureless mound. massacre background / dog howl sound clip (0:09) / covering up ecstatic death shrieks outside my headphones. ***FLASHLAND's*** fangs sufficiently fed / become anti-human / feeling ass to leather turn chest to air / pry my eyes away from the monitor they'll sheer apart / viscera vision. my arms come up, hugging the screen tightly / heat on my cheeks / melt holes in me, *please.*

liquid crystal fence torn down. i become ephemera / thigh fat a puddle now inside black sun shaped as cuboid. fingers can't separate / cupping the lead pyramids on my chest. HER cursed to ME, ME blessed as HER. standing at the foot of the bed, butchered parents all the same. the room dark now, lit only by TV glows. the bits of brain / intestines glisten like news footage. my crotch

is still. you can't put the brains back in. the program
begins to evaporate, a tek vampire! yellow sun crests over
magenta sky. data corrupting at edges of flesh geometric.

SAFEWORD XXXXXX
SAFEWORD XXXXXX
SAFEWORD XXXXXX
SAFEWORD XXXXXX
SAFEWORD XXXXXX
SAFEWORD XXXXXX
SAFEWORD XXXXXX
SAFEWORD XXXXXX
SAFEWORD XXXXXX
SAFEWORD XXXXXX
SAFEWORD XXXXXX
SAFEWORD XXXXXX
FLASHLAND

immaterial pretenses

i.
immaterial pretense pump me up for operation
replace all my bones w/ frozen lemonade!
maybe for a few minutes before i pool onto the concrete
calling myself a girl won't
feel so fucking counterfeit

ii.
riot glows dance in the ceiling futures
phone whispering banshee at my side
consumed by a world in razor focus
silos scar the midwest ready to vomit gamma

erosion crests the periphery
desperation alienation my stilled muscles fixate
there's something new sparkling in the plaster
deja vu for a girl that'd never be

iii.
july sunset condenses in left shoulder
inferno flicker & bubblegum fader
tragic ready w/ the Tower at my nape
i know it's all sick imitation
but please tell me i'm glowing
before my muscles detonate in red shower

iv.

God, oh God
back into the negative periphery
irises aflame with static glitter
there's no hiding from fakes here

railgun love bites

burying my face in the
carcass of your kiss
decapitated memories of your smile

happy necrofitted railroad spikes cross
stitched thru the lungs / husked inside iron maiden
saturated impalement at the skull

they say touched heals but i've
teeth barbed in tungsten

do lovebites w/ a railgun heal quick?

Princess of Pink

hyena princess fur of hot pink
glittered up her side
eyes black-taped over pupils blooming electricity
muzzled trophy'd aberration
stilled up on the mantel steam bubbles
thru leather silencer around maw
doesn't deafen pain like the movies show
heartbeat sanded down a rat's rhythm now
her tears made a boy treat

bark bark barks evaporated
off her tongue inhale
her bubblegum silence

spotlight on back at all hours
sunburnt stench clinging underside

diet of ghosts
cannibalizing memory only bliss left
taste of simulated sakuras
neonblood fade in out in out
in out in out on a non-space
veranda eaten at the corners by tv snow

one foot in tampa bay
the other in lake michigan
kentucky wolves eating thru her abdomen

strongest bite among mammals
ain't worth shit
when barbed wire's strict against her tendons
grip mouth around bondage
rip & rip & rip & rip
sparks along her lead daggerteeth
shredding herself in all directions against
the axis of the comfortable state

time burned thru her head &
like a switchblade corruption
slides in she's puking forest fires
wants to see the gators frenzy
misses the acid burn
watching cranes spurt red across
reflective surfaces during
sunrise at the 10pm

ribcage like moss infestation
on the oak floorboards spine
parallel to the crawl space mud

the hyena princess needs saving
and the house is quiet

gulf stream incident

radio crackle of an insatiable need
for Systems For Arranged Living

only sense in the empty between stations
like an impatient night blood find reprieve
mixing in with noise dripping off speakers
take care of the ghosts at your feet
drone under hypnotic injury delirious oil
swimming in a diamond viewfinder

doom ghosts & missing frequencies & the pseudo-planes
caving all maps of Routine Territory
ugly & evil things are bubbling out of the gulf stream
we're all targets here

prophecy of a dying girl, movements

sexy like the creases along a detonating 120mm tank round. only voyeurs the reptile anomalies crawl on upside walls. horns gut myself dick in wound only pleasure bathed in red. azaleas blooming in dirt between cracked kevlar. exist retreated in the gap between the ribs. gurgling down the only way i see love anymore i'm dessication. hydra of silver vista off its shoulder pukes storm clouds.

reduced to the flowers i don't bloom the gashes i commit. hyperblade pressed against hard bone pressures cracks me. sparrow living in my insides w/ trauma between her beak. sakuras in my spit crack legs like branches & take advantage of me. don't resist yourself because i'm here with my paranoia ready for you.

fractals in the blood reveal themselves like metal whales coming up to breathe hot steam. ignore the half-eaten cigs between my teeth i'm a heaven in disguise. drinking snake oil sabotaged futures. black market of living things where stiletto heels cut the meat. hazmat myself against the instincts. contagions bleeding into tap water i suck down those mutations.

週刊
少年
WEEKLY JUMP
ジャンプ

semtex ads in the back of shonen magazines

val's got her brain on hotwire. equipped w/ screen-cracked iphone 6 loaded w/ trap edm dj mixes & bdsm furry porn + some crushed dexedrine tablets up her nose, val slurps ramen down her throat while midnight bluelight burns in front of her. channel 2999 oozing like melted crystal from the LCD. we've demonic terror-serpent knights on the loose. mercenary splinter factions waging forever wars in lush alleyways. a mass media that's going full tilt into pornographic schizo-breakdowns about the 7 trumpets or something.

every morning started w/ ultra blue monster energy + marlboro smooths x2 + fingering herself for 20 mins in bed + a cocktail of 30mg adderall IR & 20mg percocet. this morning she was fucking herself to the audio of 240p liveleak footage of fatal car accidents played over muted hentai vids. too dumb to torrent. she just saved what she found thru shit like /h/ & sankaku. girl trawling blurry corridors, filled w/ anger & sadness & pain & slurs & gore pics, for .webms of women getting fucked semi-consensually by dicks too big for them while theyre sobbing & passing out & sometimes dying. just enough val can atomize her impulses for a few mins. this scumfuck bitch. this is responsibility. preventing herself from going full columbine mode even if that probably only meant the "spilling own brains all over the carpet in public" part.

she was addicted to saving pics online. it was her primary activity between the rape fantasies & crushed pills. a young naked girl's skull caved in & the blood n gray matter spilled all over some concrete. save image as. screenshot of vid where guy gets three 5.56mm rounds into his chest & 2 in the jaw & begs his own blood into the sand. save image as. she loves this shit. after she's done puking from the initial shock she's soaked her panties every time. beautiful shot of a BTR-80 shitting black smoke w/ one of passengers w/ his legs crushed under the back wheels & immolated thoroughly. save image as. all in a singular folder designated w/ a random string of numbers. no categorization, just a 3,540 image deep hole burrowed into her.

val's face is made of blood. she saw this coming, whatever. just constantly pouring from her nose, mouth, eyes, a gash across the jugular. half-past bled out. the tigers are circling us now. performing holster draw drills while listening to Hello Kitty Knife by Negative XP (ft. free refills) in her head as meditation. she's no tiger, but you ever breathe in demons?

val hates too much to let herself panic. she just wants to be touched by a boy. she plays VR fuck games to make up the difference. there's this one called ***'* **** **** ****** where you pretend to be a boy flirting w/ & eventually fucking an anime schoolgirl w/ hair like sakuras. val fucks her cheap onahole softly as she tries not to let in the silence swarming chaotically in the dead apartment around her. like a cloud of anthrax. outside lethal. that was her only training. she was leaning over the anime schoolgirl [age approx. 15-16], her crotch wet as she took in hot virtual pussy. to kill hostiles & the combatants are the machinations of a world order currently seizing violently under its own blood. val cums. hot droplets that coat the back of her hand. let the nephilim & their incestuous snake children eat themselves alive. val is stockpiling spiritual weapons. current training: a book detailing 9/11 as a mass ritual in tribute to aleister crowley. she only feels frustration after fucking the anime schoolgirl. the load on her hand dries. she pretends the hand w/ chipped teal nail polish is a girl's while she cleans herself up.

regiment of blackpill hypnosis. doom nausea. #EFE4B0 background tattooed w/ #026207 text. the news media is just for footage of pretty missiles. val's jacked in to defunct websites on zombie domains that offer psychotic truths. those hyper-manic insights into deep terrors that most of us can only look at with a deflected glance. val's been receiving intel from an underground spirit network covertly leaving messages in the patterns on her carpet. psionic guerilla warfare. chemtrails are more sinister than you realize. americans should have been wearing M17 gas masks years ago. 300k dead & counting lol.

the smokescreens of our daily lives are only growing thicker. phosphorus pentoxide & bleach are the scents of spring this year & val's left iris has capabilities equivalent to a Zeus 640 2-16×50 thermal imaging weapon sight. she's known of DARPA's Project Sidewinder for a few years now. near-collapse from a contagion is just phase 1. she's never been touched below the waist before.

she's developing strategies for saving America. val was always a patriot at heart. capitalists were illuminati. board execs operate as state-sanctioned terrorists. saving America from impaling itself on the sword of Al-Qaeda again. saving America from itself & installing communism [whatever kind sounds coolest at the time] & herself. val wants to be the tyrant for once. let the girl drive a tank. crush a few torsos under muddy treads. val would look stunning w/ a gold-plated AK-47 slung across her midsection.

she's an invasive species. creature of pure reflex. handlers supply her financial needs. old school spooks from that era where they were running around the jungles of Vietnam assassinating young women. they left her messages occasionally, "how are you doing sweetie," she ignores all of them. only sees the world in cruel symbols & intense meaning. using surplus budgets from CIA black ultra-ops to buy armaments behind their backs. she needs no instigation. her face is full of blood & she breathes demons. the world is pouring gasoline on itself & she's not afraid.

how much of your pain is just ritual, val. what convinced you doom is inevitable. val loads her DD MK18 AR-15 SBR. she's dreaming of afternoon spring. its 9:38pm & the moon is cutting itself. val prepares pipebombs packed into a backpack slung over her shoulder. rifle draped along her left shoulder she hikes up onto a mountain bike. 13th birthday present. never like the other boys, but she tried. she starts biking towards a nearby National Guard checkpoint she heard about in the city outskirts. fantasizing about a suicide vest loaded w/ 3mm steel balls w/ the name of her favorite boy stitched into the chest. she got too lazy & ran out of time. faildaughter even in matters of domestic terrorism. as acid fills her muscles & her lungs burn, val is melancholic. brain foggy w/ dreams of the sensations involved in a 5.56mm NATO round puncturing thru her chest & out her back. Machine Girl type heartbeat. choke those chunks of lung. maybe she can get a pipebomb or two under a humvee & blow some weekend warrior's fucking leg off.

shivering little girl, stop that, remember you're a raptor & you've got teeth for days. she almost kissed a boy, once. 17 & a half yrs, summer. she was in the park of the town she grew up in. the cicadas were whining like tomahawks. they were sitting near the pond, half-dried up. val felt her breath eat at his neck, stray hands could tell he was hard. would it be everything she imagined it would have been.

she settles for meeting hell w/ the fantasy of his kiss & a face full of fire instead of blood. paradise doesn't wait, val.

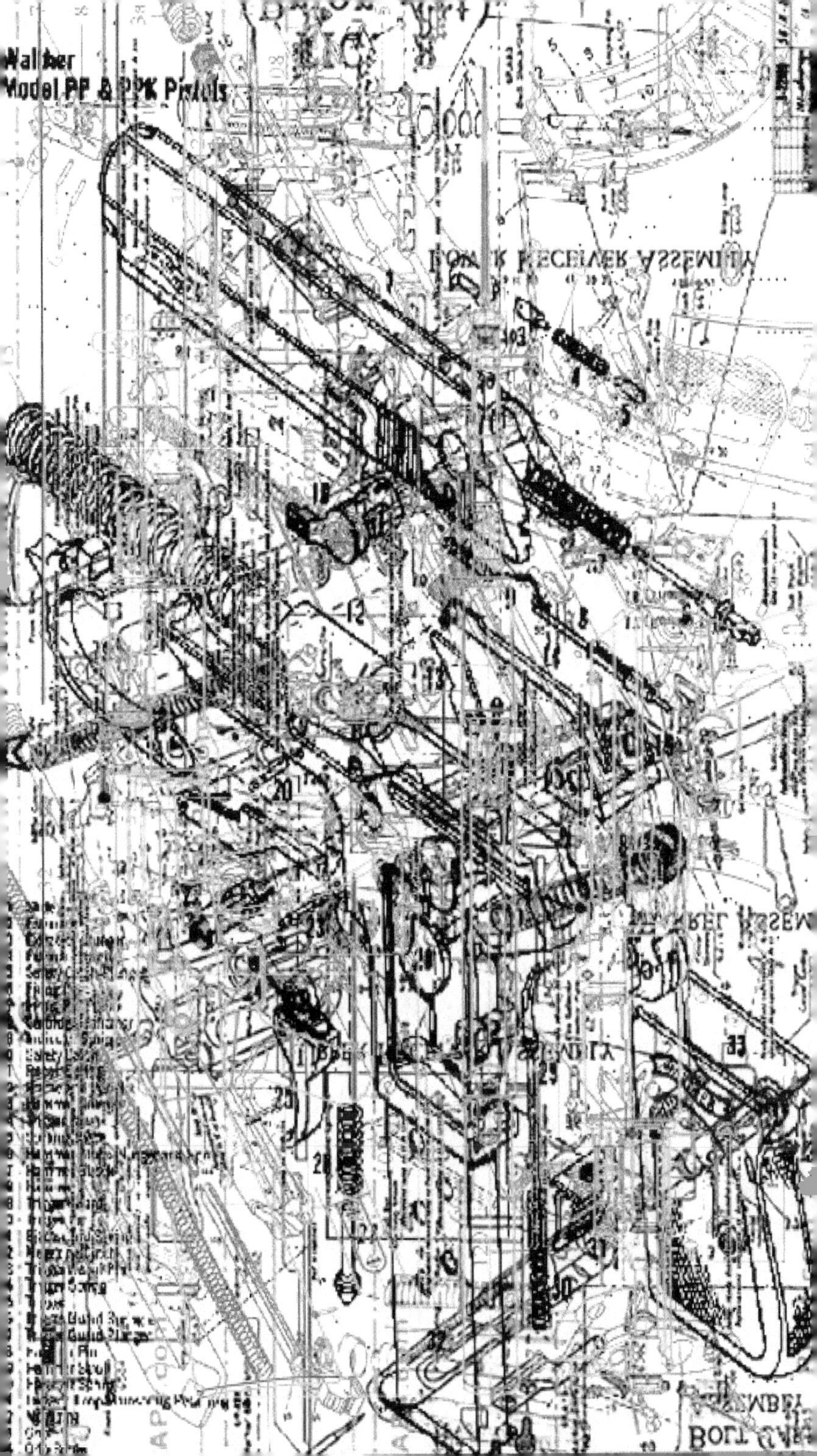

Walther
Model PP & PPK Pistols

JDAM

a village in the Syrian desert
a dozen names to the people
making water from the sand
nameless to all the spectators tuning in
to see the sand made into blood

the Joint Direct Attack Munition (JDAM)
goes kill intentions all-weather
empathy stricture along strake kits
watch heads vaporize in smokey air
unknown faces grasping at limbs
their memories drained out on dirt roads
eyes coated in monochrome nights
pupils drawn in crosshairs
precision-guided shivers down the spine
tableau of multiplying
infrared white smoke clouds

grainy torso soaked in fragmentation
beating hearts reduced to view counts
non-combatants disseminated as data
banshee yells haunting compressed audio
go-pro footage slick with red dust

fire and forget me, bitch. laugh all
you want i'm casting daggers clean
through your conscience
your headless soul

vertigo over Groom Lake

/ dizzy with fantasies of calm waters / of poetry sung at sunsets / instead jackals trespass in death valley / biting at the carcasses of shit-covered war machines / phantom fighter jets implode over restricted airspace / and the impotent channel a mandated psychosis /

/ mass arrests the new hotness / ritual castrations for the Badge / nightstick burrowed in the amygdala / reticule centered on pretend hostiles / thriving in violence markets / cracking your brother's leg on the static-washed late night news / do you feel alive? /

/ hackermancers hijacking MQ-1 Predators / sharp visions of bass-boosted calibers / The Minigun make your skull river / oscar mike into splendor flame / barbarian demolitions buried beneath military airstrips / gladio puked out into the new century covered in blood & bile /

/ there are people missing and strange, metallic figures are appearing in the sky / blurry-faced creatures are darting through treelines / uncanny lights spatter the night in blue / will we be okay? /

defective mortar shells

/ thaumaturgy in sulfur trenches / a girl left spilling red
across the bank of a Syrian oasis / Charon refuels his
humvee outside cities older than desert rot /

/ head swamped up in the dirt / inhaling lizard secrets /
sanguine knives bleed her chest / purgatory left as viscera
by paradise winds / the girl asks, can we stay on the river a
bit longer? /

/ slow-motion smoke cutting along jade eyes hung black
/ Afghan foxes spread jaw kissing treaded rubber / she's
choking on shit in a Babylon gutter /

/ death power superslice her gut / pretty scumshit puking
plastic anger / her blood splattering self-portraits on
brutal sand / she's no tiger / just paper bombs detonating
impotently in old jungles /

Detonator well
Molded, slit-type peep sight
FRONT TOWARD ENEMY
Scissor-type folding legs
Plastic matrix containing steel balls
LOST SMART BOMBS / DEFECTIVE
MORTAR S...NG APART
THE HORIZ...INFERIOR
EXPLOSIVE
INDISCRIM...UNDLESS
SHOCKWA...BODIES
SQUEEZED...FLAUGE
COYOTES FANTASIZING ABOUT
PRESSED MOLLY & DEAD WOMEN
HAUNTING A BAGHDAD STRIP MALL
CERAMIC BODIES LIQUID AGAINST
CONCRETE / PUPS DYING IN
BARREN FIELDS FOR ANOMALOUS
METALS & EMPTY FUTURES

dogs

/ young girl trapped as ***BOY MONSTER***. / dogshit head sloshing in chemicals / figure sharpened as switchblade basilisk /

/ viper hunt in a sinkhole / weather control devices burst thunder over insurgent camps / desperate to be more than ***MONSTER*** among the doomed / outlines pooling in the mud / terrible images bubbling up from a haruspex's eyes / of ejected shell casings searing ankles / of meaningless armored warfare waged over vacant plains / her chemical mask falling way to **STRUGGLE**. /

/ attack dogs recognize scents of girl underneath / **SNARL** at ***MONSTER*** / the bandit canines bark at entities hiding in perimeter bushes / from jaws cracked wide micro-knives scatter and resting crows fall, butchered /

/ dropped to her knees / nothing left but / the pooling crimson sculpting against gravel / ***MONSTER*** hunted off the Pacific coast / headline afterlife all that's left to the young girl /

STANDARD ISSUE M84 STUN GRENADE

death encoded 20yrs in // the XX defined null
algorithm determined breath amount // 1/0 toss up
i commit insignificant big-violence in Flatland
all concepts singular here
i toss out another bisected moth into the 3D
i toss out a dismembered cock into 1D

american brand survival
daggerknives to gorefuck the boyblood
by 27 i'll have fake double X's
stay execution

resort to allowing the 'don't tread on me' snake
to fuck my plastic cunt
violated on the white house green LIVE LIVE LIVE
the USMC eagle slide my tits down its gullet
pay-per-view spectacle // violation worth $$$15

immaterial expenditures // apathetic labors
ruin due i give in // i am fucking tired. i hate you

stadium-above the neon hisses:
Custom Crosshairs For
Custom Assassinations Here

opt out the death by bullet complexities
Agree To Execution of User Life Agreement

// make it bright you fucks

flashbang scraping between teeth
// a death sentence
named M84 chiseled on its hexagonal shoulder
// a less than lethal
fortuna trapped in overwound cassette
// a deflagration-processed injury
my jawbone will be hanging by the hinges
take me // bang me

last words denied i shred the ceiling with
'make me the SWAT terrordump' &
170 decibels coats across my face
glued to the gums

warthogs

kirov-class beasts crawling along the coast
piloted by revolting war shamans
puke their thermobarics on cliffsides
fear dogs! really just lost pups eating empires

& the hyenas continue dining on carrion
outside of bombed out temples
you vicious & cruel & savage royalty

warthog gunships sparkling under old sun
violence still burrows around underneath
their empty & damaged gunmetal faces

MILITARY GRADE SURVEILLANCE CAMERAS

/ mind on a spit between simultaneous psychic forever wars / 7.62 rounds glinting harshly like walmart jewelry / brass vipers spilling out of open chests / bullets cheap as blood / a Bastard paints the red room today / corpses wrapped in torn pages of an ancient codex / footage of dominations sold in black & white infrared / Bodycount Is Sustained [[17ct.]] / boy made of porcelain brushes crushed guts off his shirt / programming stored in a melting Y chromosome /

/ ponytail tied like a well-oiled semi-auto slide / dripping ghostly over sliced shoulders / uniforms [branded] strapped tightly to every twitch of the crotch / fed to burst with news that bleeds a sweet taste / channel 7 pooling onto emerald tongues / silver clinking against the back of teeth / low key heat check riot underneath / learning to puke in between an absent adolescence / witchblade etching serial numbers on missing sex organs / restriction class XXX released / a life begins in fluorescence /

 / ego bubbles up the brainscum / mercy, pity, or saved for later? / KILL INTERNAL PROJECT in all caps inside the skull / vomit fraying the air / biostatic / hickeys like cobra clung to throat / hexes escaping the bloated stomachs of dead coyotes covered in centipede shit / assassin transcending dealt divinations / outlived weaponization exiling her to New Mexico slums / Trinity sand caked on blushing cheeks /

18yr old girl[?] no longer needed to spontaneously combust enemy combatants in foreign hot zones. limbo dealt down the subject. she buys gov't nerve agents off darknet honeypots. uselessly, she says: "just dome me already, CIA!" fantasizing about a death by gunshot from the inside out. watching salvos of 80x80 pixel flame gifs fire off across a default sky. finding grace with the latest in-fashion esoterica. seeing everything as luciferian terrors filtered through bright green text on a white background. the new world order is flow time, and she wants to come home to a harem of lithe anime demon-boys! she's reverberating on, like, 7 different dimensions at all times. astral projecting herself out of a body without congruence.

before, all she had to do was let voices tell her who to kill. now the whole Dictionnaire Infernal wants a piece. Amon's dog fangs keep falling through ceiling cracks. his serpent tail flicking past peripheral doorways. turn her into Baphomet effigy.

chewing foil tablets. every bystander a sting operation. military grade surveillance cameras replacing their eyes, eating her fake image. convinced what she's packing's declassified. side-eying neighbors disappearing with fresh livers left in the sink.

/ stray lead penetrating thru crowded strip clubs [she always wanted to strut her stuff] / becoming a squatter in a half-spent minefield / CIA handler daddy has to come collect his hot gun-toting mess /

/ THE GIRL CULT DIES LIVE / hyperreality selling hot / strapping on a bulletproof vest weighted with wolf's teeth / loading glassed yokai into a mossberg chamber / canteen sloshing with chernobyl water / air thick with diamonds / drones [GENDERQUEER BODIES] like vultures buzzing her Dreamland / Hellfire strikes on the dissonant mind / shatter, shatter / Bodycount Remains Sustain [[34 ct.]] / she will prove herself even if it guts her /

DANGER LEVEL XXX CHEMICALLY UNSTABLE ENTITY. open wounds casting hypno-rainbows! bleeding new flavor!

HOT LEAD DEVILS

/ copper crown dug thru skull / a girl exists shift-to-shift / a forever humiliation / forced to regularly beg for her life / praying to false royalty to see tomorrow / demons made the regular / coral snakes around her irises / all while she grovels under boots / there's prettied up war machines on an infinite battlefield / uptempo mortars in the skybox, 24/7 entertainment always on Channel 18 / and ads at every corner, yelling, "let us make you our murder-doll!" /

/ fantasizing about shrapnel'd heads / half-stepped out the days / letting stims swim thru her skull / anarchy sparking between her teeth / grit under day-to-day / a girl ready to sin any way she can, to escape the slavery cult /

/ propane ignites under brain / another shift, another john spitting at her feet, another evening of war porn on the TV / enough! /

/ princess diablo's gold fangs glinting / she always stayed pretty for monsters! / now terror's pitching up, coated in blood spatters / damaged sky and she's ready to burn alive to taste those motherfuckers / done slutting for the Corporate / done being decimated daily for living / done tasting their false power / everyone's just fucking done! /

/ savagery stuck between teeth / gunmetal bitch slathered in red spitting 37mm bore / homemade anger chewing burnt air / and now there's wastelands in Sierra & bonfires lighting Appalachia / corrosion flicked off the tongue / saying no to the futures we were promised /

/ angels are choking on red silk now / fear the osprey / chambered talons dripping lead / devils licking blood off American sand / can't feel her fucking face / thousand deep on herself, no matter / she'll vomit her lungs before she takes another dollar with a wink & smile! /

DULCE

/ date night spent watching pink tracer rounds glancing off beer bottle curvatures / the field behind dad's garage bathed in girly fairy fires / letting budweiser aluminum bleed / ashing our cigarettes to radio wails / in-between frequencies discharging reverse reptile speech /

/ in camo flip-flops / kicking our feet up / lawn chairs suckled by magenta moss / muzzle sweeping empty-mag uzis / across the sky pretending we're nailing crow corpses to the clouds / making passing UFOs spill their guts on suburb roofs / using silent bullets (for the quiet nothing) / Mysterious Liquid Corrodes Through Local Man's Skull! / Hahahahaha! / laughing past each other looking lovingly past each other / caressing past each other / i feel like my only anchor to day-to-day is uncanny blood /

/ it's date night! / our lips rot together in soft kisses / crying melty gold into each other's throats / your beauty past all the heat / hilting you inside my jaw / slitting our chests with hollowtips / wolves covered in ancient dirt falling in love / i carved my name in your gun a long time ago /

/ draconic somethings coming to take me away from you / heel turn unloading the empty magazines / forces born off event horizons /

/ a sun from the time of sacrificial tributes swallowing me up /

i won't forget the taste of your metal behind my jaw / it's date
night, after all /

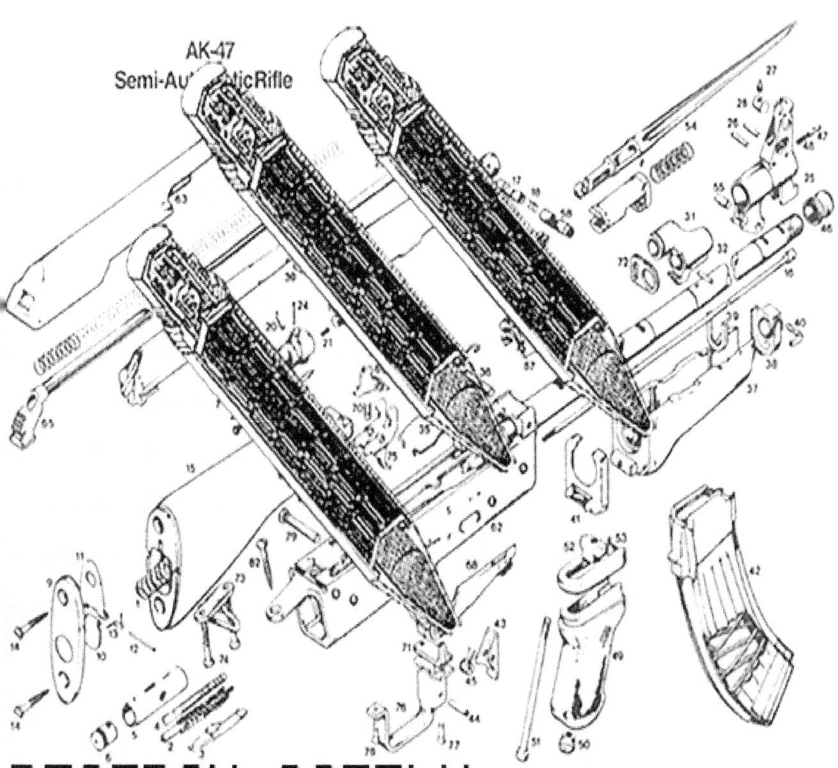

DESTROY SOFTLY

breaths between clinks
of the bolt
god let them die tomorrow

primal seizures
of the trigger
turning enemies into pelts
shimmering in the twilight
slick with organ grease

futility production
lazing around
a munition apocalypse
materiel determined fortune

devil kingdom primed towards
foreign flatlands

a living fire utilizes
surge tactics amongst
exotic ruins bunker busters
split wounds into
the earth along
ancient beaches at
1,450 ft/s (440 m/s; 990 mph)

ultrashock and awe strategies
out of limbo kill records
engraved on the side of M4's
they revel
in the bisected brains

hostageZ

rattlesnakes fucking in humid bunkers
howitzers percussive against the moss
payload discharge of ricochet razors
leaving predators tongueless

diesel bombs blowing apart windows
psychonaut long distance radars
screen past the bone
SPIKED FUZE ZEROED
thermite light the sternum

separated in hostage conditions
control terminations agency deflections
arming wire coiled around the teeth
don't let yourself turn to dormant violences

bandit logic flicks off safeties
cobras strapped with surface
-to-air missiles slither over the mesa

lethal asymmetry

here at Daytona on D-day v.7 with
young blood spilled by old methods

unfinished gunfire at the end of mixtape #4

ribcages crushed underneath star-spangled treads
drums fat with petrol
bitten in half on the mud
those god blessed bulldozers
raging endless in Persian killzones

operators slick with glass
detonating plastiques in towers older
than the sand & juvenile machines
rolling through dune tears
petulant insects crawling no purpose
shitting death along monochrome landscapes

hacker assassins wanting to eat themselves stupid
with things like honor valor integrity pride
patriots! my face is hazy with dreams of
full-auto rifles w/ drum magazines
sighted on their paper spines
pretty shink of charge handles
the teeth of the powerless
sharpened into tanto blades

AS GOOD AS DEAD

/ muddy kalashinikovs glinting in the high sunlight / passports to the Sahara dealt in 7.62x39mm cartridges / i'm good as dead / a useless martyr bleeds out on the savanna during a sunset massacre / shallows of spent brass casings and splintered wood /

/ snapping serpent spines over my maw / shooting up sharpvenom / gut shot colors bleeding over the lips / my name is weighed in hot steel / violence alchemy / under hypnosis of death visualizers / transmuting heavy blood into plastics /

/ hostile entities circling like a wolf pack / bizarre creatures of slate faces / atrocity voyeurs weaponized for maximum spectacle / i can see murky sniper pairs moving into position / bounding mines hopping into throats of recon units / sublime rending of flesh / dealing deadly to the death merchants / combat elixirs seeping through my stomach /

steppe monsters

a full metal kaiju draped in ammo belts
craters dirt with its talons / slit eyes glassed over
charcoal forests line its spine
apaches wielding molten knives strafe
the black underbrush / figures with
slung over shotguns crouch in dark smoke

a girl's stomach deforms
and tears around a lead slug
in the shadow of invisible prisons
she's speaking in red now
SHUTDOWN SHUTDOWN
gasping out futile whimpering
to have her head split

hyenas are eating carrion
outside bombed out temples
i will die for nothing and
i will kill for everything

the Flak Wolves perish on the first sunset of winter

wolves in body armor howling at nothing. hungry hungry hungry HUNGRY. eating and killing and shitting for **********. siege upon their own ramparts. **HUNGRY.....** being filled with sizzling holes in a prayless landscape of hollow figures dotting the hills. a manic pack commander, clung to by a glittery coat of maroon and a diesel-powered automachine for her right leg, is feasting on her own offspring. she is codenamed KARE. in their war, even the puppies are soldiers. Kare reflects: *the enemy uses weapons of all ages. trained from birth for death. all is opponent.*

they all wear dog tags, stamped in blood, with a single designation: *FACTION*. flat trophies of silver, displaying meaningless names devised for the smooth operation of endless combat. her tags flaunt the name of her highly-trained spec-ops barbarian tribe, *FLAK WOLVES*. platoon of beasts that only live for a full kill feed!

the Flak Wolves are a squad of doomed canines. nameless and absent meaning in their fangs, only the pack commanders are given names beyond expressions of disgust. the wolves have no kill count. each head they tear is forgotten. only clung to their memories by scents. killing and being killed. they're life inverted. only born on their own death. they'll keep hating and hating and hating and hating until the world is empty.

an exchange managed by blind/deaf wolves spews out pointless rewards none of them murder for. the money is deposited directly into accounts many of the furred mercs forgot the details to years ago, banks some of them bombed the fuck out of long prior. they were fighting for the thrill of the **KILL**, now.

while the blade between her jaw is sinking into collarbones, she finds herself projecting into memories of a past that might have never happened. hallucinatory shades. lavender under her lips. lovers from the wastelands, scarred and tired. whoring for more meat, raw and bloody. she fucks in her head and fucks her head. dopamine overflows her brain. pleasurepleasurepleasure as bones separate.

she was whole, once. before the acid rain. now her brain only stops burning when seeing her reflection in puddles of combatant blood. fragmented against a stray flechette lodged in her temple. **ONLY MASSACRE REMAINS**.

a pelvis cracks between her front teeth. she's supine against a slate floor, the inside of her bunker. eating her young and those of her squad never felt good. it never horrified her. it was *necessary*. they never stopped spilling organs and they never stopped fucking. fuck anything that moves, dead or alive! carnal addictions ravaged the group as much as lust for death. it was the pack commander's job to clean up the leftovers. can't raise new blood towards a canceled future. small livers slithered over her tongue. **CRUNCH**. the floor is wiped clean of carcass. only a spattering of viscera left. she laps it up.

Kare surveys over fields of her beasts performing training exercises against a red-tinted sky. the sun is starting to lose itself earlier and earlier. the snow will be here soon, she thinks. UFOs of blinking green are splaying across the horizon. Kare realizes, we've got hostiles. we've always got hostiles. fuck! a .50 BMG round shot from the trees turns the upper half of one of her valuable hacker vv()lv35 into worthless & gory lawn decoration. ribcage hung taut out the cavity.

she barks orders to the scattering canines. enemies at the treeline are making their way through the ranks like blood from open wounds. a rival faction has come to collect. the debts they all owe each other, in [dead] body weight. knife fights in the sun's red grace. Kare could see her support gunner, the one that always held impenetrable walls of suppressive fire with his back-mounted chainguns, surrender to the combatants. they gave him so many new holes he could barely feel how empty his body suddenly became. a war crime. **A MEANINGLESS DISTINCTION FROM ALL OTHERS**.

her troops have scattered too much. the radio chatter is just laughing ghosts. Kare runs back into her bunker, holy place of arms. on the westward wall hangs the tank-like apparatus her support gunner used. **THE SUN IS SETTING**. the barrels spin a little as she slides the behemoth onto her back. comforting, the feeling of cool metal of a war machine on her fur. memories of home. metal sheering against metal. this is her church, her place of worship. a landscape where every day is the Sabbath. make sure the ammo boxes [filled w/ 7.62x39mm w/ tracers every fifth round] are slotted into place. the machine is operated by a grill connected via wire that she bites onto for particular commands. left bite to reload. jaw splayed open in cries to fire. her revelry is shattered by two of the enemy wolves sneaking into the entrance of her bunker. they don't even get to see the bullets that reduce them to paintings on the wall. only heard the whine of six spinning barrels whining.

Kare coats the left side of her head in their blood on the wall. the inevitability of it all. she will enjoy herself, dammit! her unit is falling apart, their dog tags littering the ground. her sniper team is at her feet, all their legs torn off like paper at the knee by shrapnel, lifeless muzzles pressed against each other. the Flak Wolves are finally receiving sentence. death for the ghouls. the sky is turning royal. she, and the rest of the company, won't last until nightfall. few minutes at best.

she's the pack commander, 437 high-caliber rifle rounds on her back, she will dance! whore herself for the raw and bloody once more! bury me in the mountains, she requests. they are ravenous tonight, won't be much left to bury. live the hour in the minute. suicidal tensions. high-octane melancholia leaking out of bullet holes. more enemies heads' blow apart like pinatas full of red-stained ribbons. bathe that battlefield. as she sinks her machete under a shoulder blade her mind wanders to that phantom past. caressing a lover under the nightshade, long rotted. i want it, she says. please.

ON-SITE
死んだロシアの
THE FLAK WOLVES
戦車装甲モジ ON-SITE

FULLY AUTOMATIC SANDSTORMS

coyote-fanged warfare infinite under jungle
cracking arachnid abdomens over the tongue
letting the seconds stretch like my pupils
TV's bubbling out of the trees scum footage on repeat

lead moss taking over my face
respite in snake bite pleasures

streetlight under tree canopies
fluorescent wails silencing the titanium birds
heart on tripwire
POINT THIS SIDE TOWARDS ENEMY
we're all trapped on a stationary earth

it was always going to go down like this
knew their deck was stacked yet what
could they do but let it ride
after all bullets are cheap
i don't think the price ever mattered

let the desert eat the trees i breathe kill zones
fully automatic sandstorms climax on the mesa
cactus needles made of hollowpoints
a living fire suffocates in death valley
i'm the voyeur monk sinking below the rocks

12 gallons of mixed viscera—organs/bones

spill from nowhere
onto the bottom of the Grand Canyon
a passing lizard bites into metal shot
wrapped up in a shredded tendon
let god sort the gore out

there are quiet nukes going off
the coast of Singapore

a girl under the black gutter screams
turned into red condensation
on the front of a riot shield

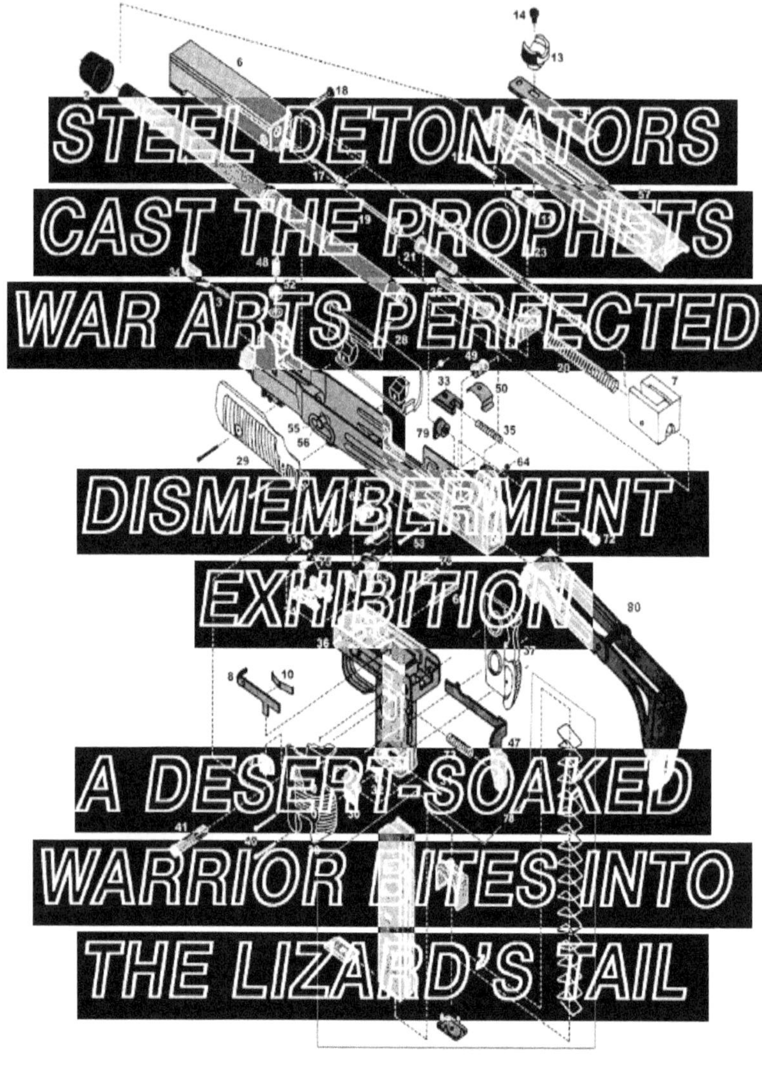

STEEL DETONATORS
CAST THE PROPHETS
WAR ARTS PERFECTED
DISMEMBERMENT
EXHIBITION
A DESERT-SOAKED
WARRIOR BITES INTO
THE LIZARD'S TAIL

Mika is a trans experimental writer from Indiana. She tweets about blood and military weaponry @tokyo_vamp and runs the online literature project Surfaces.cx.

www.ingramcontent.com/pod-product-compliance
Lightning Source LLC
Chambersburg PA
CBHW061919130726
47908CB00017B/2599